ALICE MIRANDA

Credit,

What it could mean to you

Copyright © 2024 by ALICE MIRANDA

All rights reserved. No part of this publication may be reproduced, stored or transmitted in any form or by any means, electronic, mechanical, photocopying, recording, scanning, or otherwise without written permission from the publisher. It is illegal to copy this book, post it to a website, or distribute it by any other means without permission.

ALICE MIRANDA asserts the moral right to be identified as the author of this work.

ALICE MIRANDA has no responsibility for the persistence or accuracy of URLs for external or third-party Internet Websites referred to in this publication and does not guarantee that any content on such Websites is, or will remain, accurate or appropriate.

Designations used by companies to distinguish their products are often claimed as trademarks. All brand names and product names used in this book and on its cover are trade names, service marks, trademarks and registered trademarks of their respective owners. The publishers and the book are not associated with any product or vendor mentioned in this book. None of the companies referenced within the book have endorsed the book.

First edition

This book was professionally typeset on Reedsy.
Find out more at reedsy.com

Contents

Introduction	1
Credit Card and What You Need to know about them	2
The truth about Balance Transfers	5
Balance in your Credit Life	8
The best way to use our Credit Cards	11
Our Homes are not a piggy bank	13
Refinancing and PMI	15
Making the most of our Refinancing	18
Reverses Mortgage and What You Should Know	22
Conclusion	25

Introduction

*W*elcome to, Credit: What it could mean to you. My name is Alice and I am writing this book to give some insight. I want to help you understand the fine print that comes with your credit cards and home loans from one layman to another. The stories I share are true and we had to learn this the hard way. Not by being educated but by living it. If I could help one person from having to go through something close, would have done what I could. I can tell but I can't make you make better choices.

 A little background, I am a bookkeeper and I took care of my father when he got sick. That is the only reason I became familiar with his credit situation. Had I known what he was thinking earlier, I would have made sure he didn't close any of his accounts.

 Years later My Mother's home of 60 years went into foreclosure due to her refinancing. It seemed that I was putting out one fire after the other. Not because we were doing anything wrong, but because we didn't have the needed information. She didn't know what she didn't know. I know we are not the only ones. I am not a credit specialist or a mortgage broker. But I know what we have been through. My book is a quick read with valuable information. My goal is to make you think and rethink. I am sure there is a gold nugget in here for you and your family.

Credit Card and What You Need to know about them

First things first, we all need credit that is a fact. How many credit cards do you have in your wallet? And do they all have a balance on them? What is your interest rate? What do you use your credit cards for? Do you know the answer to these questions?

Are you using your credit card for the bonus? Example: I have a credit card that gives me points with my purchases and with these points, I can get gift cards. Last year I had enough points to get $400.00 in gift cards which I gave away at my Annual Christmas party. Sounds good, right?

The truth is I paid $2.720.00 in interest. I know I am not the only one who has done this. Do you see my point? I could have put a little aside every month or bought one card at a time purchasing the cards for $400.00 and not paying $2,720.00. Because the reality is that's how much I paid.

Other cards give you cash back. But are you paying $ 1,000.00 in interest plus fees a lot of these cards have annual fees to get $100.00 in cashback.

Example: you can earn $250 after spending $3000.00 on eligible Purchases within a certain time frame. The key here is "eligible". What if you spend all this money on some purchases that aren't eligible for the cashback? Another thing to think about is $3000.00 at 20% interest is $3,600.00 did you think about it?

You could get $250.00 but it could cost you at least $600.00 in interest if you don't pay it off every month. The truth is a lot of these cards are 27% interest and up

Now to be fair some cards will give you $250.00 for spending $1,500.00 in a certain time frame. But these are welcome offers.

This is different from what you will get after, the first 6 months are over. You will only receive 1-3% cash back on eligible purchases, most cards have a max in the calendar year. If you can even reach the max. okay, there is a max on how much you can earn but not on how much you will have to pay in interest. For some this is wonderful but if that is not you, understanding your card can save you a lot of money. Have you been coming out ahead?

Or how about the credit card that gives you points for miles that's a good one right? You need to know if there are blackout dates. Is there an annual fee? Are you even able to use the miles? Will life permit it at this time in your life? Which Airlines have poorly valued miles? Do you spend enough to take a trip using only points or do you have to pay half points and half cash?

This sounds good because you only have to pay half the amount. Right? But some cards only allow you to use their site, you can't shop for a better price and all too often you could have found a flight at another site at a better price.

CREDIT,

How much interest do you have to pay on that card to get enough points to go anywhere? Think about it. Look at how much interest and financial fees you paid on your December

statement and compare that to the cost of the Airline tickets. 9 out of 10 people paid more interest on that card than the cost of the tickets. Why?

The truth about Balance Transfers

Cards that have no interest for 6 to 18 months if you transfer your balance to them. Sounds good right? Did you know if you transferred $10,000.00 to a card with no interest for 6 months you would have to make a monthly payment of $1,667.00 to make it worth it otherwise you will be paying interest on your remaining balance.

$10,000.00 in the 18 months you would have to make a payment of $600.00 or again you would be paying interest on the remaining balance. Most card companies will give you a minimum payment due of about $29.00. They don't want you to pay off the balance in 6 months. Or even the 18 months therefore you are right back where you started but now you are paying the new company.

Right? Or are you? Did you think about the transfer fee which is about 4% which means your $10,000.00 Is now $10,400.00? If you paid the minimum payment of $29.00 for the first 6 months you would have paid about $174.00 which doesn't even cover the transfer fee. But if you paid the minimum payment of $29.00 for the 18 months you would have paid about $522.00. Yes, that covered the transfer fee but not much more.

And the card that you transferred the balance from how many times

CREDIT,

did you use that card? In most cases, you now owe even more than you did when you started. And now you have to pay for both cards. Can you see the web that credit can wrap us up in if you misuse it?

There are always two sides to every coin. Transferring your balance will give you 6-18 months to pay them off interest-free but you must pay them off in that time frame. Now if you can't pay the whole balance, pay as much as you can because it is still interest-free.

Remember any remaining balance you will have to pay interest on., And most differently don't use the card you transfer the balance from. Do not close it, just put it away, and once a year make a small purchase on it to keep it active and keep you in good standing.

You don't want to close any of your credit card accounts because we do live in a credit world and not having credit is the same as bad credit. In the credit world.

Example: My father sold his house therefore he had no mortgage for over 8 years, owned his truck no balance due, and didn't believe in credit cards. Did feel the need for them. He paid everything with cash. Can't go wrong with Cash, he would say. He was debt-free and retired with a good income.

One day he came across the new Dodge Charger, a muscle car my dad called it. And for the first time in a while, he decided that he was going to have to deal with a car payment for a few months until he could pay it off. He had $15,000.00 he wanted to use as a down payment. However, the dealer turned him down due to a lack of credit. They told him he would have to get a cosigner. Which was mind-blowing because he had purchased 2 homes and several cars in his lifetime

THE TRUTH ABOUT BALANCE TRANSFERS

He had closed all his credit cards. He paid everything off. He was now debt free, therefore he did not think he had to worry about his credit. He had good credit until he didn't. No credit is the same as bad credit. Once you close your accounts they show as closed. The report doesn't show why they were closed, it doesn't show that you had good credit for many years, only that they were closed. And after a few years, you no longer have credit. Regardless of your lifetime achievements.

Balance in your Credit Life

We need to have a balance in life, not having credit holds you back but having too much credit takes away your freedom. And all your money. Unless you are one of those people who have a money tree in the backyard. You need to be credit-wise.

Think about all the interest you are giving your credit card companies; do you think you can think of a better way to spend that money? Now it doesn't matter how much you make, it's how you can keep.

Correction, having too much credit isn't bad. Using too much credit is what can hurt us. The better your credit the more offers you get, all the companies want to give you cards and or loans. I was once told "If they are dumb enough to give me the credit, I am going to use it" Example: This person was paying $435.00 a month, the minimum payment, and the card was maxed out at $20,000.00 he never really paid attention to the interest. He didn't even realize he was paying $418.00 a month in interest. He had been paying the minimum payment for over 10 years.

That is somewhere in the ballpark of over $50,000. in interest. It would have taken him a lifetime to pay it off. His credit was good, he made good money. I am sure he could have used that $50,000.00 in a much better way.

BALANCE IN YOUR CREDIT LIFE

I just saw an ad the other day for a credit card for "BAD CREDIT". Yes, that's right, bad credit. Credit Cards are a big business. Now if you are in this situation with bad credit. Please know that if they know you have bad credit your interest rate will be astronomical

There are other ways. Some cards help you build or rebuild your credit, and it wouldn't clean out your wallet. Be wise, be informed.

There is another kind of credit card. You have to be cautious with the retail and or department store card. Most have an interest rate of 28-29%.

Did you know the average person will spend more if they have credit than if they were using cash? Example: You need a pair of jeans that are about $60.00, but you have an open balance on your card, so you get a shirt for $32.00 and a pair of shoes for $40.00. They're on sale!

Your $60.00 trip has now more than doubled. $186.00 with taxes and interest. If you don't pay the balance in full your $60.00 jeans are now $84.00 and going up each month. Let's say you are not like the average person, and you go for the Jeans and only get the jeans. Your $60.00 jeans if you don't pay the balance in full. Looks like this:

You pay your minimum payment of $29.00 on your balance:
- Month 1- $84.37 -$29.00 ($60.00 plus 9% taxes +29% interest)
- Month 2- 71.43 -$29.00 ($55.37 plus 29% interest)
- Month 3- $54.73 -$29.00 ($42.43 plus 29% interest)
- Month 4- $33.19 -$29.00($25.73 plus 29% interest)
- Month 5-$5.41- $ 5.41 ($4.19 plus 29% interest) Now you only have to pay a

CREDIT,

Now you only have to pay a $29.00 minimum payment so you will be fine. Right? Your jeans cost $121.00. And took over 4 months to pay in full. Question: Are you the kind of person who didn't spend anything more in those 4 months? That's great if you are.

But wait, the next birthday or holiday is just around the corner, what will you be spending then? Think about it, only you know.

The best way to use our Credit Cards

The best thing is to pay off your balance monthly therefore you will not have to pay interest on your purchase. If you use it for a larger item and can't pay it off at the end of the month, pay it off within 6 months, never pay the minimum payment or you will never be able to get out of debt.Another thing is, to try and keep the balances of your card low. Credit monitors suggest below 30%. But remember you are paying interest on your monthly balance every month. Until you can pay them off.

Don't look at your total debt, it could be overwhelming. Each card can be paid off at a different rate.

How do you eat an elephant? One bite at a time. That's why we don't look at the big picture or we may think this is too much to eliminate. It's not, you can do this!

Now you need a plan, know which cards you are going to pay first and in which order for the next one. Now I am not saying this is going to be easy, but it will be worth it. You could also try paying your payment early if it is due at the end of the month. Paying it in the beginning or middle of the month making a mid-cycle payment will save you money on the interest. Because it is calculated based on your average daily

CREDIT,

balance.

The first step to getting out from under all your credit card debt is to start by paying them off one at a time. First, the smallest balance then put it away but don't close the account.

Now whatever you were paying on that card, use that money and add it to the payment of the next card, which should be the card with the highest interest rate, and so forth until you have paid off all your cards.

Now some would say pay the Highest interest rate first, but I say the smallest balance first when you first start because once we have paid off one, you will be surprised by how good it feels. So, unless the Highest Rate is also the lowest balance. Do the smallest balance first. Otherwise, it may take too long to pay it off and you might get discouraged and give up.

Yes, you are focused on the card you are paying down but don't forget your other cards. You need to pay them on time and if possible before the due date, and also try to pay $5.00 over the minimum payment, this will help you increase your credit score as well.

Remember we don't close our cards when you pay them off. The credit is good, it's just not being used at this time.

We live in the real world, if something comes up and you need a little extra money and have to pay just above the minimum payment, do it just that month, so you don't have to use your credit cards, and the following month go back to the plan of getting them paid off and becoming debt free. If you mess up, don't give up. Start again and get back to the plan. You got this!

Our Homes are not a piggy bank

First, we have to remember our homes are not assets, it is a liability until we pay them off, and we don't own them. If you don't believe me, stop making your payments and see if the bank doesn't take it. Liability is not an Asset.

Equity, we like the sound of that, right? All too often we use our home like a piggy bank. Take out money all too often.

In the same way, Equity goes up with the market, it also goes down.

Did you know that for the first 10 to 18 years or so we are not even paying much principal, mostly interest, and if you sell your home or refinance within the first 15 years. Which a lot of homeowners do. You have to start all over each time. Not many people think about that. We live in a time where we don't concern ourselves with more than the here and now.

This is a good one. We try to be responsible, and we use the equity in our home to pay off our credit cards and other debt but don't stop using the credit cards. So, again we have twice as much debt. Our mortgage payments are now higher and most likely our interest rate is higher as well.

if you didn't know most companies charge higher interest for a loan where you take out money. Can you see the hole we are digging? Now Refinancing doesn't have to be a bad thing if we use wisdom.

Use the loan for what it is intended for to get yourself out of debt. If there is no other way. Now if you have refinanced your home in the past but are now back in a lot of debt don't keep using your equity of your home.

This is what so many people do. By doing this we are not removing the debt, it's still there but now it's adding to the cost of your home. Did you know that a lot of people will owe more on their home after 10 to 15 years of ownership than they did when they bought it due to continuous refinancing?

What is the definition of insanity? "Doing the same thing over and over and expecting a different outcome."

Use the loan for what it is intended for to get yourself out of debt. If there is no other way. Now if you have refinanced your home in the past but are now back in a lot of debt don't keep using your equity of your home.

This is what so many people do. By doing this we are not removing the debt, it's still there but now it's adding to the cost of your home. Did you know that a lot of people will owe more on their home after 10 to 15 years of ownership than they did when they bought it due to continuous refinancing?

What is the definition of insanity? "Doing the same thing over and over and expecting a different outcome."

Refinancing and PMI

Here is another thing to keep in mind if you refinance your home to get out of debt and or to take out money for any reason. But you didn't do any calculations, and you didn't realize that you will now be over 79%. Say, there was a drop in the market, or this is not the first time you refinanced your loan, or your mortgage lender is an amazing salesperson. Doesn't matter why the results are the same.

You could end up paying mortgage insurance known as PMI on the home you have been living in for years. Don't fool yourself this insurance isn't for you. The insurance is to compensate the lenders in case of a default. That means your mortgage payment goes up, but it doesn't affect your principal or your interest balance. So, you get to pay for insurance that you will never see the payout for.

Here is something else you might want to think about once you have a PMI. Your mortgage company won't even think about removing it for 10 years. Even if you have paid enough to get you under the 80% LTV (loan to value) it will not go away. And don't think that if the market goes way up, they will count the increase. No, that doesn't work either.

Mortgage Insurance is added to your payment when you first buy your home and don't have the full 20% down payment. The home is new,

CREDIT,

and the leader doesn't know if you are a good risk or not. The truth is they are not in the business of taking risks. Therefore, they make sure they have the securities AKA Mortgage Insurance.

The sad truth is when we refinance our home it doesn't matter if you have been in your home for 1 year or 50 years if you go over the 80% LTV you will be paying for mortgage insurance. You would think after being in the home for many years they would consider that and know you don't want to lose your home. Nope, it does not work that way.

Unfortunately, more and more seniors are refinancing their homes for what they call home improvement loans. This is another way of using the equity in the home. The loan companies don't care that the homeowner is in their late 60's or 70's. And will most likely never be able to pay off their loan.

Example: I know of someone who needed a bathroom remodel. It was as old as the house 65 years. The salesperson was amazing. I was told they were friendly and knew what could be done. So, she went with what they said. Sounded like a dream come true, by the time he was done. There was a bathroom remodel a new roof and a $125,000 bill.

Now you might be thinking to yourself, that's good but the home is only 1200 sq ft. Had she been educated, or had asked the correct questions? She would've realized she didn't need a loan that high. She overpaid, for that price, she could have added a new bathroom and still have her old one remodeled. She could have added another room.

The sad truth is we are now seeing more and more seniors fighting to keep their homes. They are still paying mortgage payments in their golden years 80's and 90's.

When they should be enjoying life. Watch out for the seniors in your family. I truly believe they are being targeted.

I know of too many seniors who are given a home improvement loan in their later years. They worked their whole life and most never dreamed they would end up paying for their home for the rest of their lives. Some have been in their homes long enough to have paid them off twice. Bottom line: Our homes are not a piggy bank. We can't keep taking money out of it. It will catch us, you may not think so, but it will

Making the most of our Refinancing

I would try a personal loan or a debt consolidation loan first. This way you have one payment at a better interest rate.

Example: If you have $10,000.00 and are paying 28% interest. On your credit card. Your debt is $12,800.00. But with a debt consolidation loan the interest rates can run from 6-8% depending on your credit score, so $10,000.00 at 8% interest, your debt is $10,800.00. You have already saved $2000.00, and it should be paid off in about 3 to 5 years.

Now if the loan has an interest rate that is in the same neighborhood as your credit cards. Stop, and go back to the first plan paying your cards off one at a time. The truth is interest rates are kind of high right now. Do your homework to make sure you are getting the best loan.

Now if your credit isn't good due to high balances. If you can't get a good loan, stay with our first plan and pay them off one at a time. Stay focused on the one and remember you don't want to pay the minimum payment on the rest, it doesn't matter if you only pay one dollar over the minimum it is still favorable.

The whole idea is to have a better chance of getting out of debt. But again, stop using the credit card, I can't say this enough.

Delayed gratification is not something you hear too much about these days. We want it now. And we don't care how we get it. We used to use lay-a-way and or saving up for what we wanted. Those days are long gone. Where did they go? Credit was supposed to make life easier. But we have gone so crazy with it that it has done the opposite for so many people. Especially our seniors

Here is food for thought, If we have to refinance to pay off our credit cards or to get home improvements. Your Mortgage is now for 30 years again. This is why so many of our seniors are still paying their mortgages in their 80's and 90's.

All the years you have been paying are wiped out and you have to start over. Or do you, if you are going to refinance look into fewer years instead of another 30 years why not look into 20 years? If you can get a good interest rate that is a good way to go.

Especially if you have been in your home for a while remember you don't need to take all your equity out just because it is there. The idea is to get out of debt and get a newfound freedom. You want to be able to enjoy your golden years and not have a mortgage because at this point, if you are a senior, you are now on a fixed income. That's a fact!

If fewer years is not an option, why not add extra principal to your mortgage payment? You paid off your other debt whether it was a loan or credit card. The money that went to that could be used to pay extra principal on your mortgage.

- If you pay an extra $100.00 you can pay off your mortgage 21 months faster.

- If you pay an extra $200.00 you can pay off your mortgage 36 months faster.
- If you pay an extra $300.00 you can pay off your mortgage 55 months faster.
- if you pay an extra $400.00 you can pay off your mortgage 69 months faster.
- If you pay an extra $500.00 you can pay off your mortgage 81 months faster.

You get the picture. You can take years off your mortgage just by being credit-wise. Instead of paying interest on your credit cards, use the money to take years off your mortgage.

Yes, you have a 30-year loan again due to the refinancing but let's work on paying it down faster.

You might also think about using some of your income tax return money, if you get some to make an extra payment of principal to your mortgage every year. Or how about your annual bonus, maybe not all of it but some of it. Put some of it to the principal of your home. Truth is when we get extra money the last thing, we think about is paying extra on our mortgage.

One extra payment of principal a year can take 48 months off the life of the loan, and the extra we are adding to our monthly payment can take off more years. So, when you get to your golden year you won't have to fight to keep your home. Credit is so overused that we don't get to retire debt-free, we get to pay to the very end. Well, that is not for me, and I hope it's not for you either.

MAKING THE MOST OF OUR REFINANCING

We need to learn from the errors of those ahead of us, and not walk into the same mess.

Reverses Mortgage and What You Should Know

One other thing to look out for is the reverse mortgage, which is fairly new, and more and more seniors are having to turn to this because they can't keep up with the payments or they just want more money to enjoy their golden years. Now, if you don't have any family that you want to leave your home to, it is a good option.

However please be aware this is another mortgage that is very hard to get out of. Okay, if down the line you decide that you don't want to give up your home. You can't just refinance your home. You have to qualify as a new buyer to keep your own home.

I found out about my mom's reverse mortgage when I received a letter informing me that our family home was in foreclosure. When I asked Mom what was going on, she said she didn't have to pay the mortgage anymore. Due to the new loan. Of course, I got Power of Attorney to be able to go over all the finances and not have to worry about her creditors speaking to me.

When the salesperson sold her on the reverse mortgage. He also sold her on another home improvement loan. Being that she didn't have to pay a mortgage payment anymore, she could fix some things in the house. Or just have some extra cash.

Now, they did use the house's equity, but they didn't add to the mortgage. There were 3 loans in total she was still paying for the new bathroom and a new roof. The new payments came out to be more than the original mortgage payments. And it was at the cost of her home. When I explained to her what she had done she asked me to save her home.

I asked the mortgage company about what would happen, and they said we would not take the home. You will have a chance to sell it. I even went so far as to speak with a lawyer, I was told that we basically signed over our family home. That is a reverse mortgage.

As of right now, we won't be able to repurchase the family home because we all have our mortgage payments. So, we will most likely sell like many other families, but I don't believe there will be any equity left in the home. I can't save our family home, but I did promise I would make sure she would be able to live in it for the rest of her life.

Things you should know if you have someone living with you and they tell you that you need to be living alone to qualify, walk away. If you have someone that you want to add to the deed and they discourage you, walk away. If they tell you that they are going to give you a credit line, that way you can do repairs to the home. (For the new owner) or to have extra cash.

Look to see if you are at 80% LTV. They can and will add Mortgage Insurance to a reverse mortgage. Please get all your facts before Refinancing or doing a reverse mortgage. It could cost you, your family home.

Anything that you have to make a monthly payment on is a liability, not an asset. And will remain that way until it is paid in full. Which means if it is a house they can foreclose on it. If it's a car they can repossess it.

This is why so many people are losing their homes because they think of it as easy money, an easy way out of debt. But they are not eliminating their debt, they are just moving it along.

I get many calls every month to inform me that I could take out my equity to pay off debt go on the vacation I always dreamed of, and or do home improvements. Now if I am getting these calls know there are many more receiving the same calls. Perhaps even you. We as consumers need to make better choices.

Conclusion

Everyone needs credit. Not knowing and understanding our credit is bad. Our house belongs to the mortgage company, our cars belong to the bank. Therefore, they are liabilities, not assets, for as long as we are making payments. We should act like it. Credit is good, but how we use credit could be very bad for us today and in the future. No credit is the same as bad credit, using too much credit at once is also bad.

We use credit for travel, entertainment, and all too often for our daily wants. Yes, I said wants not needs. Everyone needs credit, but what we don't need is to live on credit. Having credit and living on credit are not the same.

My hope, if nothing else is, I can open your eyes to the world of credit. I am sure you have heard" Too much of a good thing isn't always good". Now let's work on understanding where we are and where we need to be, freedom awaits us.

If you found this book informative in any way, I'd be very appreciative if you left a favorable review for the book on Amazon! Thank you

www.ingramcontent.com/pod-product-compliance
Lightning Source LLC
Chambersburg PA
CBHW071000220526
45471CB00007B/3108